Junior High Library
Brandywine Public Schools
Niles, Michigan

Janet Lynn
sunshine on ice

Janet Lynn
sunshine on ice

BY LINDA JACOBS

EMC CORPORATION
ST. PAUL, MINNESOTA

Library of Congress Cataloging in Publication Data
Jacobs, Linda.
   Janet Lynn, sunshine on ice.
   (Her Women who win, 1)
   SUMMARY: A biography of a professional ice skater who at age twenty signed a three-year contract with the Ice Follies for almost a million and a half dollars.
   1. Lynn, Janet — Juvenile literature. [1. Lynn, Janet. 2. Ice skating — Biography] I. Title.
GV850.L96J32 1974 796.9'62'0924 [B] [92] 74-2133
ISBN 0-88436-122-5
ISBN 0-88436-123-3 (pbk.)

Copyright 1974 by EMC Corporation
All rights reserved. Published 1974

No part of this publication can be
reproduced, stored in a retrieval
system, ro transmitted in any form
or by any means; electronic, mechanical,
photocopying, recording, or otherwise,
without the permission of the publisher.

Published by EMC Corporation
180 East Sixth Street
St. Paul, Minnesota 55101
Printed in the United States of America
0 9 8 7 6 5

WOMEN WHO WIN 1

JANET LYNN ★ SUNSHINE ON ICE
OLGA KORBUT ★ TEARS AND TRIUMPH
SHANE GOULD ★ OLYMPIC SWIMMER
CHRIS EVERT ★ TENNIS PRO

WOMEN WHO WIN 2

WILMA RUDOLPH ★ RUN FOR GLORY
CATHY RIGBY ★ ON THE BEAM
LAURA BAUGH ★ GOLF'S GOLDEN GIRL
EVONNE GOOLAGONG ★ SMILES AND SMASHES

WOMEN WHO WIN 3

MARY DECKER ★ SPEED RECORDS AND SPAGHETTI
ANNEMARIE PROELL ★ QUEEN OF THE MOUNTAIN
ROSEMARY CASALS ★ THE REBEL ROSEBUD
JOAN MOORE RICE ★ THE OLYMPIC DREAM

WOMEN WHO WIN 4

CINDY NELSON ★ NORTH COUNTRY SKIER
ROBYN SMITH ★ IN SILKS
MARTINA NAVRATILOVA ★ TENNIS FURY
ROBIN CAMPBELL ★ JOY IN THE MORNING

Lights dimmed in The Forum in Los Angeles. Thousands of chattering voices fell silent. The audience waited.

"Ladies and gentlemen," a voice on the loudspeaker said, "the Ice Follies is proud to present the skating artistry of Miss Janet Lynn."

The lights turned pink. A small blond girl swooped onto the sparkling ice. Her pixie hair bobbed around a smiling face. She twirled and jumped. "Sunshine on ice," some people called her. Three thousand pairs of hands applauded.

Janet Lynn had started her first performance as a professional ice skater. At age twenty, she was ending one kind of life and beginning another.

Janet's amateur skating career was over. She would no longer skate for medals and awards. Now she would skate for the sheer love of skating. But as a professional skater, she could finally earn money for her talents. And what money! When Janet signed her three-year contract with the Ice Follies, she became the richest woman athlete in the world. The contract was for almost a million and a half dollars.

What makes a 20-year-old girl worth that much money? Talent and hard work, that's what. Many people think that Janet is the best woman free-skater in the world. The people who know her best are quick to agree. And they do things to prove they agree.

Janet's parents spent the money needed for lessons and for trips to amateur competitions. Skating judges named Janet the United States Ladies Champion five times. Former Olympic champion Dick Button agreed to manage Janet's professional career. The Ice Follies signed her to that big contract.

But nice people doing nice things didn't give Janet a free ride to success. She earned that ride through a love of skating that began when she was only two-and-a-half years old.

At that young age, Janet put on ice skates for the first time. It was a winter day on a frozen pond in Chicago. Janet had tagged along on a Cub Scout outing with her older brothers. The little girl looked like a chubby doll, wobbling across the pond. She fell many times. Sometimes her chin would quiver.

But she always got up. She tried again and again and she wouldn't let anyone help her. By the end of the day, Janet had stopped falling so often. There were many more skating outings that winter and soon Janet had even taught herself how to skate backwards.

Two important things happened because of that first outing. Janet's parents saw her talent and Janet herself discovered a love for the free-flowing motion that was ice skating. From that time on, her parents really had no choice. It was give Janet skating lessons or listen to her pleas as she begged, "I wanna skate, I wanna skate!"

Fortunately, Janet's parents could afford to give her the lessons she wanted. Her father, Florian Nowicki, owned a drugstore in Chicago. He was happy to pay for the lessons. So skating doors opened for a toddler named Janet Lynn Nowicki. Soon she was on her way to becoming the star people now know as Janet Lynn.

Janet, the star, dances her way to another skating championship.

Janet began class lessons right away. At age three, she passed up everybody in her class. At three-and-a-half, she outskated a class of teenagers. By the time she turned four, Janet was beyond class lessons and ready for a private teacher.

But Janet's talent for skating was not without its problems. One problem came when Janet was three-and-a-half and already in the teenage class. The students were asked to write a report on skating. Janet couldn't even write! That one was easily solved. Janet simply drew crayon pictures and passed the course in good order.

But there was another problem that had bothered her since she had first started skating. Just trying wouldn't solve that problem. Janet couldn't force herself to get over her shyness. When she first began to skate in front of audiences, she cried before every performance. At ice shows, Janet sat in the lobby. She cried because she was afraid to go out in front of people.

Her teacher or one of her friends had to talk to her. They encouraged her. They dried her tears. They got Janet in front of the audience. She always came through. She always smiled and twirled and gave the people sunshine on ice.

Other problems were harder. The hardest of all was finding teachers for such a talented girl. Before she was five, Janet outgrew several teachers. Each one taught her all he could. Then it was time for Janet to move on. Finally, there was nowhere for her to go — at least in Chicago. It seemed she might be stopped — not because she didn't have enough talent, but because she had too much.

The famous Janet Lynn smile lights the skater's face as she relaxes off the ice.

Then, one weekend in 1959, the Nowickis took Janet to the famous Wagon Wheel skating center in Rockton, Illinois. There she met and skated for the well-known skating coach, Slavka Kohout.

Miss Kohout raved about Janet and was eager to teach her. She saw a natural winner. Janet had grace and an excellent sense of balance. Those were things that couldn't be taught by any coach.

Miss Kohout wanted Janet and the Nowickis wanted Miss Kohout. Everything should have been perfect, but it wasn't. Rockton was over fifty miles from Chicago — too far for a daily drive. And Janet had to work every day if she wanted to compete for skating medals.

The Nowickis thought about the problem and talked about it. Florian Nowicki had a busy drugstore in Chicago. His business and Janet's skating just couldn't get together.

Then Mr. Nowicki did a wonderful thing for his daughter. He sold his business in Chicago and went to manage another store in Rockford. Rockford is near Rockton, but it is a bigger town. Mr. Nowicki felt he could someday start his own business there, too. The Nowicki family moved to Rockford.

Soon, the family was settled and doing well. So was Janet. With Miss Kohout's help, she began to work hard at skating. She practiced drawing slow and perfect prints on the ice, getting ready for school figure competition. She practiced swirling, twirling dances, getting ready for free-style competition. Janet would have to do well in both kinds of skating to win medals.

Janet's coach, Slavka Kohout, helps the nine-year-old skater get ready for one of her first competitions.

She loved the dancing of free-style, but she didn't love the slow, difficult school figures. In school figures, Janet couldn't jump and spin. She had to trace circles and loops on the ice. Then she had to study the figures to see how she could make a more perfect print.

Miss Kohout made Janet work extra hard in school figures. Janet knew she needed the work, but she couldn't help not liking it. She forced herself to work on the school figures. She just tried hard.

Janet hard at work practicing the difficult school figures which she never learned to like.

During that first year of working with Miss Kohout, Janet took the first important step toward her skating career. At six years old, she got her membership in the United States Figure Skating Association. That meant she had to begin to pass the eight difficult tests in school figures, the part of skating Janet liked least.

Passing the tests in her weak school figures wasn't easy. Each test was harder than the last. Each one called for more and more work. Janet found that work discouraging. She wanted to spin and jump. She didn't care about drawing perfect figure eights on the ice. But finally in July, Janet passed the first big test and got her membership in the USFSA.

This marked the beginning of many things for Janet Lynn Nowicki. For one thing, it began her skating life as simply "Janet Lynn." Janet's coach and parents agreed that using that name would be simpler. Nowicki is a hard name for some people to pronounce. Also Miss Kohout just thought Janet looked too delicate for such a big last name.

Soon, the little girl who skated like a dream entered her first real competition. It was January 5, 1961, and Janet was seven years old. Her mother and her coach traveled with her all the way to Troy, Ohio.

Janet was the youngest skater there. She came in thirteenth out of twenty. Her school figures had held her back. Because she placed below eighth place, she didn't even get to do her free-skating. The young skater was heartbroken, but she made up her mind not to let it happen again.

The Troy competition began the real work of Janet's skating life. Back home at the Wagon Wheel rink, she worked harder than ever on those tough school figures. Her free-skating programs, too, took a lot of practice. But that was the part of skating she loved.

Usually Janet practiced six to eight hours a day. She skated before school, after school, and sometimes after dinner. She went to bed early. Every night, she got eleven hours of sleep. She watched her eating and stayed away from treats.

Finally, the years of hard work and practice paid off. At the age of twelve, Janet won the Junior National Championship. She was one of the youngest in the competition.

Twelve-year-old Janet skates her way to the United States Junior Ladies' Championship.

In Grenoble, France, for the 1968 Olympics, Janet gets in some practice time before the Games begin. At fourteen, Janet was the youngest member of the United States Olympic skating team.

For five years after that, Janet kept winning the National title. She also competed in the five World competitions and two Olympics. Janet Lynn went to her first Olympic competition in 1968 in Grenoble, France. She was only fourteen, but she did well for the United States Olympic skating team.

Taking time out for some fun while on tour, Janet tries to make friends with some bashful chimps.

All these years, skating kept Janet so busy that it was hard for her to think of anything else. But she didn't want to be one-sided. She wanted to be a whole person. Skating didn't stop her from finding time for other things.

Janet was a good student in school and she made the National Honor Society. She liked swimming and horseback riding and gymnastics. She was in as many church activities as possible.

At work or play — always a skater. But this time it's roller skates.

One of her favorite pastimes was writing to pen pals all over the world. She liked writing letters and she liked learning about the lives of other teenagers. Janet enjoyed her letter friends. But she didn't lock herself up with pen and paper. She made friends in her own home town. The old shyness didn't stop her. It was almost gone.

"I guess I started coming out of my shyness little by little as I got more involved in skating and school," Janet says. "I also started realizing that friendship is a two way street and even though I was shy, I could still try to reach out to others — even with a smile."

People reached back. Her father now owned his own drugstore again and it became a favorite meeting place for the kids in town. Janet went to dances and parties and football games.

Lots of boys asked Janet out. But they were usually awed by such a famous girl. They liked to date her and they liked her as a person. But they couldn't forget her skating and neither could Janet.

Sometimes that made real problems. Once when Janet was a sophomore, she asked a boy to a Sadie Hawkins dance. They got there at 7:15. People had started dancing. Everyone said "Hi" to Janet and her date.

Janet barely managed to smile. She had a problem. She was trying to figure a way to tell her date that she could only stay fifteen minutes. She had to get a full night's sleep before training the next day.

But Janet never worried too much about boys. She was popular; she had dates and friends. That was enough.

Even with her busy schedule, Janet found time for parties and dances.

She relaxed and acted like herself. She tried to be friendly so people wouldn't feel strange around her. That took a lot of friendliness. Janet wasn't exactly like the other kids in school. Every time she turned around, she won another honor.

Janet was a hit in the 1972 Olympics in Sapporo, Japan. She didn't win the gold medal, but she did win the Japanese people. They loved her blond, bobbed hair and her bright smile. They liked her so much that special reporters came all the way to Rockford to write about her. Janet still gets letters written in Japanese. She has to get a Japanese friend to translate them for her.

Sunshine on ice, Janet skates her way to the bronze medal at the 1972 Olympics in Sapporo, Japan.

Returning home to the United States after her Olympic victory, Janet is welcomed with a huge trophy presented to her by the city of Chicago.

All the attention made Janet a heroine in Rockford, too. The kids in school bragged about her. They often seemed surprised that someone so successful could be so nice.

"Everybody likes her," said a girl friend. "She's just great."

Everybody in Rockford did like Janet. The City Council honored her by using her picture on the official city auto sticker. They had to get special permission from the U.S. Figure Skating Association to do it.

Janet thanked them. She liked seeing her picture around town. But she never once bragged. She remained her sweet and friendly self. Maybe that's because of the way she felt about skating.

Skating isn't just medals to Janet. She was never a cut-throat competitor. She cared about other people and she had other interests, too.

Janet wouldn't let skating make her selfish. She tried not to let her problems make her sad. She kept her balance in life as well as she did on the ice.

That seems grown-up and wise for a young girl. But skating makes a girl mature. She has to discipline herself to work, to watch her eating and sleeping habits. She has to stand up under the strain of competition. And she has to learn to be in the spotlight.

The spotlight is on Janet as she turns into a whirling, spinning glow on the ice.

It isn't easy being a star. People look up to Janet. They expect her to be perfect. "People put me on a pedestal," she says. "I want to be a good example, but I don't want anyone to think that I don't have some inner struggles, trying to find out why I want to be a good example even when I don't totally feel like it. I guess it's called self-control and patience."

Janet learned that control. Her family helped her. They stood behind her in skating and everything else.

"My relationship with my family has always been very close," Janet says. "I have two older brothers — both athletes. I have a younger sister who is a cheerleader. She has taken gymnastics and modern dance. We have all helped each other.

"My parents disciplined us out of their love for us. They never pushed any of us in sports. They gave us every opportunity to find out what we liked to do. Then they got involved in helping us do our best."

Mrs. Nowicki made all of Janet's costumes. She traveled to competitions with Janet. It was hard work for Mrs. Nowicki because she also had Janet's two brothers, Larry and Glen, and her sister, Carol, to take care of. But she loved Janet and so she found time for all her family.

Both Mr. Nowicki and Janet's maternal grandfather, Gus Gehrke, followed her career, too. Her grandad, who is 79 years old, is her biggest fan. He knows every win and every loss. He knows what the papers are saying about Janet. Win or lose, he's always proud of her. And Janet knows she's really done well when her grandad gives her a big hug after a performance.

Janet's whole body moves to tell a story as she dances through her free-skating performance.

Waiting to go on, the shy skater thinks about the performance she is about to give.

Her family and outside interests helped Janet through the stress and strain of competition. Something else helped, too. Janet discovered a deep religious faith. She had always gone to church. But one Sunday something special happened.

Sitting in church, Janet listened closely to the sermon. It made her cry. It made her want to do something more with her life. Then and there, Janet promised God that she would look for that something more.

Over the years, Janet's religion helped her in many ways. It helped with her shyness when she started praying before performances. She would feel peaceful after praying and ready to go on.

Religion didn't make Janet a sour puss. It didn't make her go around preaching to everybody. It just made her happy and more concerned about others.

It certainly didn't ruin her sense of humor. Janet isn't even above thinking of pranks; she just doesn't often do them. Once, she wanted to organize a strike of all the skaters at Wagon Wheel Rink — on April Fool's Day, of course.

And Janet likes to tease Slavka Kohout, her coach, about a "turn-about." She would like to be the coach with Miss Kohout as her only pupil. She dreams about that for one reason — so she could say, just once, "Okay, that was fine. Now do it one more time!"

In the fun times, Janet bubbles. But she has her bad times, too. Then she cries and hurts like anyone else.

One of Janet's worst times came during the 1972 Olympics in Sapporo, Japan. Janet had practiced and practiced. She had dreamed of winning first place — the famous Olympic gold medal.

This was the most important competition in Janet's whole skating career. She wanted to do her best — more than she had ever wanted it before. But when the school figure competition was over, Janet had placed fourth. She was shattered.

Back in her room, Janet cried and cried. Then she prayed. She still had the free-skating competition ahead of her and she still wanted to do her best.

As Janet began her free-skating the next night she felt wonderful. She knew that God was with her and she skated to show the great love that she had always wanted to show through her skating.

Bronze medal winner Janet joins Karen Magnussen and Trixi Schuba on the victory platform at the 1972 Olympics.

Then, as Janet whirled into her flying sit-spin, the nightmare happened. Janet fell to the ice. She had done this spin for years and had never missed one. But now, at the most important moment in her skating life, something went wrong. Janet jumped to her feet. She finished her program. And even the fall couldn't take the joy from her skating. The audience loved her.

When the final scores were announced, Janet had placed third in the 1972 Olympics. She had won the bronze medal for the United States, but not the gold medal. A lesser person might have sulked. Not Janet. She swallowed her disappointment and flashed her famous smile.

Taking a quiet moment alone, Janet wonders about her future on skates.

But being a good sport didn't stop Janet from wondering about whether she should keep on skating. She was tired and depressed. After coming home, she could hardly practice. Once, she went to the rink to work for a three-hour practice session and only stayed ten minutes.

Janet began to think about quitting, but she couldn't decide. She might have wailed and whined. Instead, she prayed. And she came to believe that God wanted her to keep skating — at least until after the 1973 World competitions.

So, in spite of being tired, Janet stepped out on faith. Miss Kohout and Mr. Pierre Brunet, Janet's newest coach, tried to make practice cheerful. They wanted to help Janet with her decision. They wanted her to win and to be happy.

Pierre Brunet was a skater who was famous for his good figures. He had become Janet's special coach for school figures in 1971. At that time, Miss Kohout decided that Janet needed extra help with school figures. Together Mr. Brunet and Miss Kohout had helped Janet get ready for the 1972 Olympics. Now they helped her through a difficult time in her career.

Once, Mr. Brunet, who is well past 70, started clowning to cheer Janet. He promised to skate rabbits or roses or four leaf clovers on the ice. It was impossible, but he managed to make a good imitation.

Then Miss Kohout got in the act. She tried to skate a rose, too. Then everybody looked at it doubtfully. The figure didn't look like a rose at all. So Miss Kohout announced that she had skated a daisy instead!

Janet laughed and felt better. Then she got back to work. She kept going even on days when no one had time to joke.

Miss Kohout understood Janet's struggle. She knew a skater's fears. She knew the fear of falling on two thin blades. She knew the fear of failing and the fear of the audience.

In Bratislava, Czechoslovakia, for the 1973 World Championships, Janet gets in some practice time on her school figures.

Janet mastered her fears. In 1973, she went to the World Championships in Bratislava, Czechoslovakia. She was the favorite to win. Everything looked perfect. She did beautifully in her favorite free-style and she even did well in school figures.

Then she had to do something new. A short program called compulsory free-style was added to the requirements in the 1973 competition. Each skater had to do a series of certain spins and jumps. Of course, Janet had practiced for the new program.

But it didn't feel natural; it didn't feel free. She fell — not once, but twice. Long years of training had taught Janet to get up and keep going. She couldn't let a fall stop her. Janet trembled inside, but she finished her routine. Her eyes brimmed with tears as she went back to the girls' dressing room.

Disaster strikes. Losing her balance, Janet falls as she presents her compulsory free-style program at the 1973 World Championships.

Then an amazing thing happened. Every girl in that room started to cry — to cry for Janet. Karen Magnussen, the girl who won first place, cried as hard as the rest.

Everybody had wanted to win. But they all loved Janet. It hurt them to see her hurt. Nobody had time to be jealous. Everybody just shared Janet's misfortune.

Even with her falls, Janet's performance was so good that she won second place overall. And she won something else — she won peace of mind. The other girls showed her that she had real friends. Her prayers told her that she had God.

Of course, it had hurt Janet's pride to fall. But Janet believed everything had some purpose — God's purpose. She prayed — and the pressure she'd felt all year went away. It had been a hard year, but now she had a sense of completeness.

In this new frame of mind, Janet faced a decision. Should she continue as an amateur or go professional? She also thought of quitting skating to become a missionary. Again Janet prayed about her decision and thought about it. It wasn't an easy one to make.

She thought of the 1976 Olympics. It seemed a long way off. But she felt a responsibility to her country. She was the finest woman skater in the United States and she **would** like another chance at Olympic gold.

Then she thought of her tiredness. She thought of her parents and all the money they'd spent on her skating. It would be nice to do something for them. It would be nice to make money for a change. It would also be wonderful to do something for God.

Packing for still another trip, a thoughtful Janet wonders if it isn't time to slow down and take time for other adventures.

Janet decided that there were young skaters coming up who could take her place in amateur competition. She decided to turn professional.

"I feel that God wants me to skate," Janet has said. "I can reach people that way. And I can use some of the money I make to help others."

35

Her decision made, a happy Janet Lynn signs her first professional contract as Mark McCormack, one of her agents, looks on.

Former Olympic champion Dick Button helped Janet plan the move. He helped her make the decision to sign with the Ice Follies.

When Janet finally signed the contract that made her a millionaire, everyone said she had a great future. People said she skated as well as Sonja Henie.

That was a compliment to end all compliments. Most people call Sonja Henie the greatest woman skater who ever lived. They loved her because her skating made magic. She was also pretty and charming. Those same people love Janet Lynn for the same reasons.

All of them agree with Dick Button's words about Janet: "A great skater is one who has made the sport better and different for having been in it. Janet's skating is like a poem. She has free-flowing movements and jumps that spring up like fountain sprays."

Of course, Janet likes all the praise and she is glad to be making so much money. But being a professional skater is important for another reason. "I will be doing shows almost every night," she says. "But I'll only have to practice a little each day. It will give me a chance to do other things."

At last she can spend time just having fun. She can do more church work and make more friends. She wants to do many other things. She wants to skate and make speeches and give time to her family and friends.

Janet has many plans for her new life. She has already written a book called *Peace † Love.* It is Janet's own story of her career and of her deep religious faith.

The girl whose strong legs carry her over ice is interested in children who aren't so lucky. In 1973, she was chairman of a regional fund-raising drive in Illinois for United Cerebral Palsy. She staged a special amateur show to help raise money. Skaters from all over the country came to help her. They called it the "We Love to Skate with Janet" show.

In the future, Janet plans to use some of the money she will earn from skating to continue helping the handicapped. And she not only raises money for crippled children, she also spends some of her extra time visiting young patients in the hospital.

Janet also plans to do religious work. Already, she has made a trip to Japan for the Language Institute for Evangelism. In 1968, she went to Sapporo as an Olympic contender. In 1973, she returned to speak for her faith in Sapporo, Tokyo, and Osaka. "I try to show love to people," she said simply.

Janet does show love, on the ice and off. Perhaps that is why people love **her** so much.

Audiences admire Janet Lynn, the dancing, spinning Ice Follies star. Friends and family love Janet Nowicki, the shy girl who works hard, cries sometimes, and prays often.

Everybody agrees that Janet is special. She is talent and charm and love — sunshine on ice.

ACKNOWLEDGMENTS
PHOTO CREDITS
Black Star, 22; Jerry Jung Associates, 18, 19, 20, 21, 26, 30, 35, 37; Margaret Williamson, 24, 27, 33; Peter Travers, cover; Shipstads & Johnson Ice Follies, 7, 39; Skating magazine, 16; United Press International, 9, 11, 13, 17, 23, 29, 36; Wide World Photos, 14, 32.

The author and publishers especially wish to extend their gratitude to Janet Lynn for her assistance in helping to make this book a true reflection of her own story.

Junior High Library
Brandywine Public Schools
Niles, Michigan

DATE DUE			
NO 9 '79			
NO 28 '79	AP 12 '9?	SE 10 '01	
DE 3 '79	JA 06 '95	FE 22 06	
JA 21 '81	JA 31 '95		
MR 23 '8?	NO 21 '95		
OC 25	JAN 16 1996		
JA 25 '83	JAN 26 1996		
SE 19 '90	FE 10 '9?		
DE 17 '90	AP 28 '9?		
JA 22 '92	NO 11 '97		
FE 28 '9?	SE 11 '00		
	MR 10 '00		

B
Nowi

COPY 1

Jacobs, Linda
Janet Lynn: sunshine on ice
X47975

Junior High Library
Brandywine Public Schools
Niles, Michigan